Arthur Edward Waite

A Lyric of the Fairy Land and other Poems

Arthur Edward Waite

A Lyric of the Fairy Land and other Poems

ISBN/EAN: 9783744776516

Printed in Europe, USA, Canada, Australia, Japan

Cover: Foto ©Thomas Meinert / pixelio.de

More available books at **www.hansebooks.com**

A Lyric of the Fairy Land,

AND

OTHER POEMS.

BY

ARTHUR E. WAITE.

LONDON:

J. E. CATTY, 12, Ave Maria Lane,

1879.

GILBERT FLEMING, *Printer*, 68, *Red Lion Street, Holborn, London, W.C.*

CONTENTS.

---

iv.

A LYRIC OF THE FAIRY LAND.

I.

When first mankind defiled the heart with crime
The gentle fairies sought a happier clime,
Far, far beyond the sunset's golden gate,
    And there await
The gradual dawning of a milder time.
They linger still within those distant places,
These wondrous children of the infant world;
  Oft in the silence of a summer even
      You see them standing on the enchanted shore—
  The ruby threshold of the western heaven—
Their feathery pinions furled,
And the pale pureness of their lovely faces
      Will haunt you evermore.
Their distant palaces behind them gleam,
      Rich with a thousand towers
      Above the opal sea :
Silent they stand, like wanderers in a dream,
  And through the evening hours,
      From their eternal city,
      They gaze in pity
      On thee and me
  Toiling through the lonely hours.
When will the day come bringing them o'er
Yonder dim ocean to this far shore,
With an end to our sorrow in light-hearted laughter,
The tempests passed over and sunshine thereafter ?

The morning light expands above our heads,
　The evening sunsets fire the sky,
The melancholy moon her radiance sheds,
　And whitens in the heavenly spaces high ;
Our eyes made dim with labour's bloody sweat
Look for the promised time whose glories dawn not yet.

II.

Trust me, my brothers, there are fairies still,
　　Though seen to day no more,
And dwelling distant on a better shore ;
They have but vanished from the haunts of men
Until the golden age return again,
But now the good time goeth from the earth,
With all its guileless merriment and mirth ;
The lust of gold usurps affection's throne—
Not worth but wealth the only passport known ;
Rebellion's brood begets the foulest crime,
　　The flags of anarchy are all unfurled,
The lawless spirit of an evil time
　　Subverts the grand old order of the world.

III.

What glimpses in this dreary night
Tell of the earth's primeval light,
　　When first of God begotten ?
While idle dreams our souls engage,
The glories of the golden age
　　Are all, alas ! forgotten.
Our eyes grow dim with toil and tears,
Hearts darken with the dust of years,
　　No voice our pains can number :
We yearn for peace while cries of war
Prolong their notes from shore to shore—
　　The dead alone can slumber.
Green waves the grass above their heads,
Its silent dews the morning sheds
　　With eastern lights unfolding ;
The perfect peace has dawned for these,
Who sojourn under Eden's trees
　　The smiles of God beholding.

IV.

This earth of ours is red with blood
　　And hearts are hard as stone,

And wisdom makes us cold and proud
  With purer feelings flown.
The world goes seeking truths unkind,
  And all the fairy brood
Are driven from out their leafy haunts
  And greenwood solitude.
Yet still some hearts renew their youth
  When spring-tide leaves are green,
And warm beneath the summer sun
  And azure skies serene :
Some voice is whispering peace and hope,
  And tidings strange and good
In angel language often heard
  But seldom understood.

v.

The fairy broods will come once more,
  The elves again be seen :
'Tis only the heart of man grows old
  For the earth is always green.
Some kindlier influence still makes soft
  The hardest, harshest fate,
And joy shall cure the wounds of woe
  Ere balm can come too late.
Though evil powers prevail awhile
  And evil deeds abound,
Though lawless might oppress the weak
  And right go forth discrowned,
Yet lose not hope, some happier age
  Most tranquil and most sweet,
Shall make for all existing wrongs
  A compensation meet.

vi.

Our hopes are high for future days,
  Their comes a milder time,
When men shall walk in gentle ways
  And simpleness sublime.
The mighty past behind us lies,
  The future dawns in light,
New aims and aspirations rise,
  New truths make clear the sight.
Far on the glimmering verge of time
  We see the end of sin,

Our eagle star renews her prime,
  The better days begin.
A stormier age may intervene,
  Misrule may reign awhile,
But through the distant clouds is seen
  The heaven's eternal smile.
Oh! while the tempests round us beat,
  Star of the brighter day,
Rise—while we toil with bleeding feet,—
  Shine on our thorny way.
Hope for the hopeless, perfect peace,
  Breathe in our hearts, oh! star;
Bid the wild cries of faction cease,
  Herald of heaven afar!

THE INVITATION TO FAIRYLAND.

There is no joy for those who act a part
      In the world's noisy mart;
There is no peace in nature's solitude
For those who on the chance of merchants brood;
The heart is hardened by this greed of gold,
And in prosperity is proud and cold;
      It is no goal nor gain
If ships of ours make traffic o'er the main;
A little peace of conscience proveth more
      Than wealth's increasing store;
Under green leaves and summer woodland bowers
Is fairer resting place than golden towers;
It is a pleasanter and sweeter fate
At will to stray through nature's wide estate,
      And find, where e'er we roam,
The world is still our country and our home,
Than to find favour at a prince's court;
'Tis better with the fairies to consort
Than seek the over-peopled haunts of men;
The nymphs which haunt the woodland glade and glen,
The gentle spirits of the sylvan streams
Are better company for waking dreams,
Than with the uncongenial crowd to stray
      Where they make holiday.

Then while all day the sun shines bright on high,
And the rose blooms beneath the cloudless sky,
While the green leaves adorn the fruitful trees
And fragrant scents pervade the languid breeze,
And when the twilight deepens into night
The large soft moon ascends the heavenly height.
Ye wanderers through the meadow and the grove,
We fairies ask you in our realms to rove,
Ye dreamers by the fountains of romance,
Ye bards that roam in visionary trance,
While suns are warm and still the skies are bright,
And no storms comes with desolating might,
Let us to flowery meads and blissful bowers
Where fancy revels through the golden hours.
Through blissful realms awhile at will we'll stray,
Where shadow never mars the endless day,
Where waveless oceans spread their waters wide,
         Gently in barks we'll glide,
And reach at length some wild and wondrous shore
Held fast by beauty's spells for evermore.
Sometimes we'll linger in the humble dell,
And castles bound by many a mystic spell
Shall rise before us with their towers of gold,
Bathed in the sunshine of the days of old.
The tedious hours shall pass in music by,
No shades of evil wander grimly nigh,
But where the fairy vistas widely spread,
Our feet in charmed circles age shall tread ;
Much may we learn who seek new truths to know,
And haply gather wisdom as we go.

THE WANDERER'S LIFE-SONG.

Through the weary grove of years,
  By the course of poisoned streams,
  Lulling to deathly lotos-dreams,
Through the mournful vale of tears,
We have wandered and have waited,
  Cherishing delusions vain,
Till beyond all hope belated
In heart-Edens devastated
  By the ruthless winds and rain,
We can hope no more, no more
  Life's great goal in time to gain.

For the twilight now is near,
Autumn past and winter here ;
And the red west-light is dying,
  And the deadly vapours rise,
While the heart grows faint with sighing,
  As we look with weary eyes,
'Mid the clouds above us flying,
  For one star of hope to rise,
For one glimpse of clearer skies.

And we wander now and listen
  To some ocean's murmur deep,
Though we see no waters glisten,
  Though we hear no wavelets leap.
Thou who rulest, Thou who reignest
  O'er the shadowy world unknown !
We have hoped when hope seemed vainest
  And toiled on with many a groan ;
Say, when we embark in silence
  Bearing neither scrip nor store,
  Shall we ply the weary oar,
Shall we reach the happy islands
  Seen by seers in days of yore,
  Or upon some rocky shore,
By no gleam of glory lighted,
Wander cheerless, cold, benighted,
  Lost for evermore ?

Shall we labour then as here
In temptation, doubt, and fear,
Or beneath the pleasant shade
By the eternal palm trees made,
The probation over, gain
Rest which here we craved in vain.

LINES.

Oh ! gentle boy,
Still as of old by thy home,
Under the green, low whispering, tremulous leaves,
And in mysterious winding woodland paths,
Still, as of old, thou walkest.
Oft have I seen thee here,
At noon retiring from the summer heat,
Stretched at full length upon the shady grass ;
The pale, sweet, meditative face of old,
And the divine dark eyes,
With their long lashes,
Turned upwards to the tall embowering trees,
That in the sunshine stand so green and still,
The warm blue sky o'ershadowing their boughs,
Which purified by Heaven's celestial light
Seem reaching up into the arms of God
And basking in the beauty of His smile.

Few are thy playmates here,
Yet never shalt thou lack companionship,
Nor wander lonely with a listless step ;
Nature is round thee in her mildest mood,
And in these solitary haunts provides
Sweet comrades for thee in the flowers and birds,
In the broad lilies of the silent lake,
The melancholy sedges of the marge,
All gentle creatures of the sylvan wood,
Whose wistful human eyes
Are raised in tenderness and trust to thine.

Sweet Nature's favoured child,
She is thy chief preceptor and thy guide,
Who shapes thy thoughtful mind,
Thy guileless heart directs,

And elevates and beautifies thy soul.
Half the sweet secrets of the world are thine ;
The mystic meaning of the murmuring winds,
The voices of the spirits in the trees,
The voices of the spirits in the grass
Are understood by thee.   These spirits speak
At all fit times to thine attentive ear,
Telling strange mysteries.

Oh ! pure and kind of heart,
With so much winningness and grace of mien,
What sweetness deep is hid
Far in the holy problems of thine eyes,
What softness strange is there,
What calm and holy trust,
What princely peace of soul,
What magic worlds of wonder and of love,
What fathomless abysses of divine
And spiritual purity of thought.

Teach me thy wisdom then,
And let the freshness of thy youth descend,
A minister of peace, upon my soul,
So long disturbed with knowledge of the world.
My brain is tired with toil,
My feet grow weary in the paths of men ;
I fain would rest awhile
In thy sweet solitudes, and here with thee—
Thy hand in mine—would wander ;
And look into thine eyes till I became
As kind, as pure as thee ;
While thy low silvery voice should haunt my ears,
Like distant music breathing from the stars.
And when the hallowed spirit of the night
Drew down in silence over land and sea,
Under thy woodbine porch
We twain should gaze upon the silent sky,
The moonbeams falling on thy noble brow,
And in the dewfall and the gathering night,
The soul of all the beauty of the earth
Should manifest its presence to our hearts.

THE HEART'S TRAGEDY IN FAIRY LAND.

A FANTASTIC DRAMA.

PART I.

Scene, The Fairy Home.—Evening.—Harold alone.

HAROLD.   Thus far imagination's wandering light
Hath led my footsteps and hath brought me—where ?
To what strange shore, to what mysterious sea ?
The twilight dusk is deepening into night,
There is strange silence in the brooding air,
          And dread solemnity.
The long green wastes extend on every side,
Exhaling ghostly mists beneath the moon,
The evening breeze upon the deep has died,
No breath disturbs the sultry heat of June.
A wanderer long through realms of doubt and fear,
I gaze in wonder round and question all things here.

(The moon rises from behind the trees, and the fairy groves become visible, with Muriel wandering in the distance.)

MURIEL. (Singing)

The maiden sat in her lonely bower in the fair enchanted closes,
The sun rose red from its eastern bed, and the dews were on the roses.
The maiden sat in the burning noon, her face by the green leaves shaded :—
Alas ! for the heart when its hopes depart, and the dreams it nursed have faded.

The maiden sat in the pale moonshine, her cheeks than the moonbeams paler ;
Each star with its crown on her face looked down, but how could the stars avail her ?
For the maiden watched for her absent knight whom her silent tears upbraided ;—
Alas ! for the heart when its hopes depart and the dreams it nursed have faded.

The maiden waited and watched in vain : her watch than her tears was vainer,
The idol she cherished has perished, has perished, and the love remains to pain her.
In the glory of battle he passed away on the blood-red field unaided :
He will come no more to the fairy shore, and the dreams and the hopes have faded.

HAROLD.   What silvery tones enchant mine eager ear ?
          What magic music on the air is borne ?
No mortal but myself I deemed was here,
          In these strange lands forlorn.

MURIEL. (approaching.) If I am gazing on a human face,
          Oh ! wandering mortal, say,
       What brings thy steps to this deserted place,
          Where no man's voice is heard by night or day ?

HAROLD.   From distant lands, without an aim or goal,
          Unsatisfied, unblest,
       A weary seeker pining after rest,
          I come with hungering soul.
       But thou who art so gentle, mild, and fair,
       Thou surely hast no heritage of care ;
       Art thou a spirit from some brighter sphere,
       Who in the shadowy twilight wandereth here ?

MURIEL.   I am not mortal though of flesh like thee,
          Poor stranger look into my face,
       No shadow of decay thou there can'st see,
          No growth, no change can'st trace.

HAROLD.   Thou art some maid divine,
       I gaze on thee, abiding peace is thine ;
       No doubts nor fears perplex thy placid mind,
       The sorrows and the pains which vex mankind
              Are all unknown to thee.
       Thine eyes unfathomable, stedfast, clear,
       Gaze round on me and upon all things here,
       And read the inmost secrets of their hearts,
       As the stars read the secrets of the sea.

MURIEL.   It is not thus with thee,
       I gaze into thine eyes and see therein
       The sorrow that is shadow to the sin,
              The weakness and the pride,
       The many passions which thy strength divide,
              The fever and the smarts.

HAROLD.   Let me approach thee nearer, let the light
          Of thine unsorrowing soul, like healing balm,
       Shine down upon me in my troublous night,
          And bless me with thine own perpetual calm.

MURIEL.   Nay seek not this for it were vain endeavour,
       Thou canst not enter in this fairy ground,
       For hands unseen repel thee all around,
       And destiny, poor friend, divides us ever.

HAROLD.   Thou hast compassion for my low estate,
          Whence art thou, sweetest maid ?

From what bright realm beyond the reach of Fate,
    Whose hand mars all things here with its destructive shade ?

MURIEL.   Within this magic bound—a wondrous land
        More beautiful than day—
    My sisters and myself, a blessed band,
        Live happily alway.
    We are the children of an ancient race
    Who dwelt with man in happier days of old,
    But his best virtues unto wealth are sold,
    And tyranny and vice the world disgrace.
            Therefore with them no more
                We wander as of yore,
    But unmolested in these groves remain,
    Where entrance none can gain,
    For many a powerful spell is woven round
    The ever fruitful ground.
            Death cannot enter here,
                Sorrow nor haunting fear,
    Yet should we wander from our fairy sphere,
            The spell that holds would break,
            The curse would overtake,
    Inevitable ruin would be near.

    But now the hour grows late, the dews of night
        Fall on thee standing in the wind without;
    The moon looks downward from her heavenly height,
        Some shelter find amid the woods about,
    Or by the bushes on the starlit plain—
    To-morrow I will speak with thee again.

PART II.

Scene, The Fairy Home.—Noon. Time later.—Muriel within the charmed circle. Harold without.

MURIEL.   Eternal bliss doth here o'er all preside
    And only varied joys the day divide,
    No storms molest, no rains nor lightnings mar,
    Where summer reigns alway and peace and plenty are.
            We neither toil nor spin,
    Nor sleep for weariness, nor wake in sorrow,
    Nor painfully the new-born day begin,
    Nor end it in foreboding for the morrow.
    But like an orbitless and wandering star
    Thou camest to me out of realms afar,

With pity for thy wants I gazed on thee,
Till pity became friendship, friendship love,
And love idolatry ;
And all at once my sphere towards thine did move,
And I, descending towards thy mortal state,
Found thee controller of my future fate,
And without struggle, or relapse, or sigh
My whole heart turned towards thy humanity.

HAROLD.   Oh ! ever gentle, kind of heart, and true,
     If from thy present and superior place
My love should charm thee into regions new,
     Amid the children of a fallen race,
And thou grown weary there shouldst pine and fade,
     A sinless stranger in a world of shame,
Oh ! what to thee would be my feeble aid,
     And where the power exempting me from blame ?
I dare not tempt thee, nor protract my stay
     To be a shadow on the form I love,
And though 'tis death to tear my heart away,
     Still from mine idol I will distant rove,
If in strong purpose thou thy mind wilt set
And save thyself by learning to forget.
Oh ! sister, sweetest sister, let thine eyes
     Lighten above me for this time, the last,
If I must wander under alien skies
     Till life's storm-tide be past.

MURIEL.   My heart, dear friend, my destiny decrees,
     Whate'er may chance unalterably thine,
Thy love has opened it with golden keys,
     And has laid bare to thee its inmost shrine.
And I have wearied of my fairy home,
Through thy wide world I fain with thee would roam
     Far from the enchanted bowers,
Whose irksome beauty doth the soul oppress,
     Whose rarest sweetest flowers
Seem sickly even in their loveliness.

HAROLD.   For love of me thou dost these dangers choose,
I dare not bid thee come, nor dare refuse ;
     Oh ! tender heart,
We must as one remain who may not part.
Then let us cast all doubt, all fear away,
     All dim forebodings of the evil nigh,
And let us rather dream that day by day
     We shall roam on beneath the sunny sky,

And when the sunset dieth in the west,
'Mid the cool winds and fragrant we will rest
On mossy banks, by cool and rippling streams,
    And in our waking dreams,
Beneath the shadow of some leafy tree,
The happy voices of the earth and sea
Shall tell their secrets to us.

MURIEL.   On yonder hill
Though all the summer are the green trees still;
Oft have I stood within this fairy bound,
One foot put forward toward the forbidden ground,
And gazing on that eminence have tried
To picture all the world that far and wide
Spreads joyfully beyond it.

HAROLD.   All is fair,
The mellow sunlight fondly lingereth there;
The gentle breeze among the trees is heard,
Sweet as the singing of an Eden bird;
There may we build in some enchanted grove
The blissful bowers of consecrated love,
Or through the woodland up some winding way
Which never ends, and past where fountains play,
        Roam onward hand in hand
All the soft summer of that pleasant land;
And when the winter brings its garments cold,
And wraps the earth in many a frozen fold,
Among the haunts and in the homes of men
With genial hearts we'll dwell, till spring's fresh birth
Re-clothe and vivify the old brown earth,
And all the happy time return again.

MURIEL. (stepping from the charmed circle.) Oh! Harold, Harold,
    Lo! I come to thee,
As the parched sea-bird to the open sea;
Thus, sweetest friend, I've longed for thine embrace,
As longs the sparrow for its rifled nest,
      As weary hearts for rest,
Come nearer, nearer, o'er me droop thy face.

VOICE.   Oh! maid what would'st thou do,
        Yet pause and think,
Thy past temerity in time review,
    Thou standest on a precipice's brink

And soon thy dizzy and bewildered brain
   Will urge thee on to thine eternal ruin,
And thou too late wilt strive, when strife is vain,
   To remedy this evil of thy doing.
Have pity, pity on thy gentle friends,
      Thy sisters once so dear,
The evil passion with thy mind contends,
   If thou shouldst fall from this thy brighter sphere,
Never can sorrow for such crime atone,
Never can power of thine repair the evil done.

MURIEL.   What conflict dire is raging in my breast,
   How shall I answer those who justly chide ?
Shall I obey in prudence their behest,
   Or scornfully deride ?
I cannot struggle with all-mastering Fate,
To alter or repent is now too late.

(There is a sound as of the breaking of a spell.)

PART III.

Scene, By the Sea.—Midnight.

MURIEL.   Dost thou no shadows in the distance trace ?

HAROLD.   I only see the moonlight on thy face,
Its cold beams fall upon thy deathly brow ;
Dost thou grow weary, art thou hopeless now ?
What darksome shadow o'er thy mind is cast ?
What bodes this dread placidity of mien ?
      Oh ! love, take heart of grace,
Behold ere long bright morn will dawn apace,
The sun returneth when the clouds have passed,
And no cloud long may dim the heaven's serene.

MURIEL.   The world shows dimly in life's fading light,
   Dark shadows round me roll,
The desolation of the eternal night
   Is surging in my soul.
Farewell, dear friend, farewell !
   I may not long delay,
I hear the uproar of the broken spell,
World-ruin ringing in mine ears alway.
'Twas but for this that we have toiled in vain,
Endured the sorrow and defied the pain.

HAROLD. Lone vigil in the midnight here we keep,
Hearing vague voices of the solemn deep.
Alas! the overshadowing sword of Fate
Descending slowly smites and pierces thee,
And me in thee. What comfort can I lend thee,
   What help from healing balm,
How from thy dreadful destiny defend thee,
   How bring thee rest or calm?

MURIEL. The hopes we cherished in their time were high,
But these are over and the end is nigh;
The star of love we marked in days of yore
Has sunk in darkness and will rise no more.
Eternal guiding and presiding powers,
   Who from your kingdoms high,
   Where never change comes nigh,
Gaze on the mutability of ours,
Mercy! have mercy! I am cold and bare,
My soul is frozen by the wintry air,
Despair more fierce than death, abiding fear are there.

HAROLD. This is some dream, too full for truth of sorrow;
   Speak to me, love, thy looks are strange and wild,
Say we shall wake to sunbeams bright to-morrow,
   Mid flowers, and birds, and breezes soft and mild.

MURIEL. We have awoken and our dream is o'er,
We twain shall dream, alas! in life no more.
I stand upon life's shore with trembling feet,
My heart with terror haunted groweth cold,
The dim beyond is opening fold on fold,
Oh! cast thine arms around me, stay me, sweet;
I would not glide adown that dreadful slope,
   Nor sail away upon that dreary main,
Where comes no pause for breath, no room for hope,
   Nor any scope for pleasure or for pain.
I would not part from thee, I fain would stay
      In summer's warmth and light,
I would not pass into the outer night,
Where no fair star makes prophecy of day;
But some great hand stretched from the abyss below
Draws me, oh! friend, and I am forced to go.
Vague, solemn, unconflicting, soundless sea,
Thy tide creeps towards me standing here afraid,
While cold intensest, and foreboding shade,
And silence terrible encompass me.

Adieu, dear friend, adieu!
To cherish hope were vain,
We shall not meet again,
For gazing into the eternal night,
Nor torch, nor starlight come to help us through,
How joyless there for both if we should meet,
Through death's dark maze roaming with weary feet!

[Dies.—A pause.

HAROLD.   So the light hath faded—faded—
So the night comes on—
And her hair with storms is braided,
And her crown of stars is gone.
Gloom is round me, gloom is o'er me,
Everywhere :
Barren fields of life before me,
Pitfalls of despair.
Vain to learn the dreadful lesson
Late, too late ;
Vain lament for foul transgression
Pre-ordained by Fate.
So the dismal story endeth,
Like the hopes so bright erewhile,
Dust with what was glory blendeth,
Oh! still heart and frozen smile.

STANZAS.

The dreams of youth are fair, dear friend,
  Bright are the hopes we nourish,
No canker-worms of care, dear friend,
  Forbid life's flowers to flourish ;
But the world goes round and round, dear friend,
  The sands of time are flowing,
The flowers will die on the ground, dear friend,
  When wintry winds are blowing.

Then while we've strength and youth, dear friend,
  And hope illumes our eyes,
Shall we strive after truth, dear friend,
  And seek to grow more wise ?
Or shall we merely love, dear friend,
  Forget the name of sorrow,
And leave to the powers above, dear friend,
  The troubles of to-morrow ?

I know not what to say, dear friend,
  I know not what to say :
What matter in life's short day, dear friend,
  Whether we work or play ?
Oh ! calmly take thy rest, dear friend,
  And I will sleep beside,
My home is on thy breast, dear friend,
  Whatever may betide.

They say the end is nigh, dear friend,
  The world has passed its prime,
And we must bid good bye, dear friend,
  To all the happier time.
They say that peace is o'er, dear friend,
  The snow-white flags are furled,
And the blood-hounds of war, dear friend,
  Make desolate the world.

They bid us all prepare, dear friend,
  The wrath of God to meet,
But we can learn to share, dear friend,
  The bitter and the sweet.
The golden time goes by, dear friend,
  The darkness comes apace,
There is no beauty nigh, dear friend,
  Save only in thy face.

Let those who will put trust, dear friend,
  In princes and in kings,
But wealth and power are dust, dear friend,
  Most miserable things;
And creeds are stern and cold, dear friend,
  Repulsive when most true,
The brightest hopes we hold, dear friend,
  Too often they undo.

May all those hearts be blessed, dear friend,
  Who dream of heaven above,
I have no place of rest, dear friend,
  Save only in thy love.
How blue so e'er the skies, dear friend,
  Beyond our reach they lie,
And I prefer thine eyes, dear friend,
  As kind and not so high.

The end of all my life, dear friend,
  Is thus to dwell with thee,
I'll waste no time in strife, dear friend,
  For what we do not see;
For that which lies in store, dear friend,
  Can be no more nor less,
Because in love's sweet law, dear friend,
  We found our happiness.

HORTATIO AD HOMINEM.

Wouldst thou the pinions of the dove
That so thou mightest soar above
The sounds of earth, the shouts of men,
And, soaring, come not down again?

Oh! mighty soul, oh! little man,
Immortal bounded by a span,
Oh! strong of will and weak of hand,
They come not at thy lips command.

Thou art condemned in pain and fear
To still toil on and suffer here,
The heir of darkness, doubt, and shame,
Uncertain of thy goal or aim.

No angel comes to bid thee raise
Thine eyes to heaven with patient gaze ;
There comes no light across the tomb
Thy thoughts diverting from its gloom.

So, like the hoarse rebounding seas,
Which vainly seek the shore for ease,
Still, half in faith and half in doubt,
Thy hands for help are reaching out.

Thine eyes look on the starry sky,
And this remains, and thou dost die,
But are the stars a pledge to thee
Of death or immortality ?

When the bright moon resumes her reign,
Breathes she, hope on, or hope is vain ?
What saith the darkness, what the light,
What of the Future—noon or night ?

To ask them all thou turn'st about ;
What is their answer ?   All is doubt !
So doubtful all things seem to be,
Thou art not sure they answer thee !

Yet give not up, oh ! strive again ;
Who knows the strife is all in vain ?
For when the waters loudest roar
We know they beat upon the shore.

Press on, press on, the skies are seen
Through crowded leaves of faultless green—
So oft to chosen souls 'tis given
Through earthly things to gaze on heaven.

A PRELUDE.

Oh ! far away into the fairy realm,
Mile after mile down what deserted ways,
Beyond the homes, beyond the haunts of men,
Alone in dreams I wandered.
No more the woodman's axe at morn was heard,
No more the workman passed me on my way,
The sound of horns, the bay of eager hounds
Had died at length : the beaten paths were left ;
And as in dreams the facts of waking life
As shadows of vexation only come,
So shadowlike, so distant seemed the world,
Which had receded miles with every step
I took into those solitudes divine.

Green grew the long, long grass beneath my feet,
Green waved the trembling trees above my head,
But all things else were steeped in silence there,
And hallowed in that wondrous silence seemed.
From out the present of the living world
With solemn footsteps roaming through the past,
From modern progress and its feverish dreams
Into the grand old order,
From stern privation and the fear of want,
From bargain-driving and the lust of gold,
From charity's unsatisfing husks
Into the land of plenty,—
Into the land of bounty and of peace,
The spring-time land, the beautiful, the free,
Green pastures for the heart, the home of dreams,
Into the fairy land.

There were green fields and woodland bowers of peace
Long winding lanes, and scented hawthorn shade,
And sweet acclivities remote from men.
No strife was there, perpetual calm prevailed,
And there were no more storms, nor any night
Nor suffering, nor sorrows, nor tears, nor cold,
Nor winds, nor oceans raving. Oh ! my friends,
It would be well if ye could reach that land,
Life's adverse chance would trouble ye no more,
Nor fortune play ye false, nor love decrease,
Nor friends prove traitor-hearted.

Bear with me, brothers, for a little space,
But late returned from those diviner realms,
My tears fast fall, my heart is weak and slow,
The interests of daily life have gone :
I come among ye as from worlds afar,
A stranger and a pilgrim at the best :
I hear the tidings of the waking earth,
The bustle, and the turmoil, and the toil,
The murmur of the multitudes of men,
But peace has vanished from our hearts and homes.

Bear with me, friends, and in a little time
My tongue grown strong to strive with human speech
Shall all the glories of that world unknown
In easy syllables of song recount.

THE MOURNER.

The distant waves in tumult roll
    How wildly on the echoing shore !
Their hollow voices fill my soul
    With vague despair, and evermore
I clasp my hands across my knees
    Beside thy tomb, the loved, the lost,
From far across the gloomy seas
Unpitying blows the northern breeze,
And bends and shakes these aspen trees,
    Till their green boughs are wildly tost ;
And to their strong molester sighing
Are the pallid leaves replying.

I think 'twere well to rise and go
Where stormy horns of battle blow,
    Or mingle in the world's great mart :
But a voice within me answers " No !
This is thine only place below,
    Oh ! broken heart !"

And should some holier thoughts arise,
And speak of bliss beyond the skies,
Saying, look up, the stars above
Are covenants of peace and love,

Then comes that voice of care again—
"Can these delude thy soul in vain,
No human hearts their hopes attain.
Look on this idol of thine eyes,
Beyond all hope it shattered lies !
Oh ! ask thine anguished aching breast,
The grave alone can give thee rest,
The house of darkness, that is best."

So I sit here and dream and wait,
And feel to hope 'tis now too late ;
Oh ! here above this dust I weep
For what is dead and not asleep,
And round me are the ocean and the sky,
The lying symbols of eternity.

A BALLAD OF THE SUNSHINE.

Oh ! the pleasant summer sun,
    Welcome, welcome every day,
Through the woodland's green retreat
Shining softly, shining sweet,
Wheresoe'er with thee we meet
    All is gay !

Like the sea birds on the sea,
    Without nestling place or nest,
We are tossed on life's great deep ;
If we tire we cannot sleep,
We can only work and weep,
    Without rest.

Through our tears we gaze on thee,
    And thou smilest from above ;
As the weary years go by,
We smile too, we know not why,
Smile upon thy smile on high,
    Full of love.

Underneath it oft we sit
    Through the waning autumn day,
And thy golden rays that gleam
Over meadow, vale, and stream,
God's sweet benedictions seem
    Breathed alway.

They are sweet, those pleasant hours,
 Underneath the pleasant sky,
And we think with happy mind,
Walking where the green paths wind,
Of that merciful and kind
 God on high.

How He guides us where we go
 With His sweet persuasive hand,
How He guards us and doth bless,
How He helps our helplessness,
Seeking through the stormy stress
 Heaven's bright land.

And we feel, since He is strong,
 It is well that we are weak,
Since upon His open palm
We can slumber and be calm—
Silent thought is sweetest psalm,
 Do not speak.

And, since all to Him is known,
 It is well we are unwise,
Well we have so small a mind,
Are so darksome, are so blind,
Since we gaze and light can find,
 In His eyes.

Then how weak and foolish seem
 Things of earth we strive about,
All the doubts and all the fears,
Vain imaginings and tears,
Oh! how foolish each appears
 Without doubt.

And how very small and mean
 Are the discords, and the strife,
All the ways the world defends,
All the gold it hoards and spends,
Which does duty for the ends
 Of its life.

And with gleaming eyes we trace
 In thy blessed light above,
Thy Creator's kindly face,
While sweet voices full of grace,
Whisper from some heavenly place—
 " God is love !"

LINES.

Very kind and gentle hearted,
  Would those eyes I love grow dim,
If perchance thy friend departed
  Where thou couldst not gaze on him?

If the voice grow still to-morrow
  If the warm heart cease to beat,
Wilt thou come with thoughts of sorrow
  Where so oft we used to meet ?

Wilt thou think the past was brighter,
  All that happy past gone by ?
That thy footsteps then were lighter,
  And more proudly glanced thine eye ?

Ah ! sweet friend, the heart forgetteth
  Very soon the loved ones gone,
Happy youth but seldom fretteth,
  Soon finds hope and soareth on.

Yet I think that thou wilt cherish,
  Some affection in thy heart,
Though the first fond love may perish,
  And the early dreams depart.

When the world is quick to chide thee,
  Thou wilt turn and think of me,
Thou wilt wish me still beside thee,
  Thy support and guide to be.

Thou wilt think when men deceive thee,
  When the trusted hearts estrange,
Of the love which could not leave thee,
  Of the faith which did not change.

No I feel what e'er betide us,
  What so e'er my fate may be,
Death itself can scarce divide us—
  Thou wilt still remember me !

THE SEEKERS.

Who there hath entered, in the fairy world?
    What seaman landed on that lonely shore?
Who in its heavens safe their sails have furled
        To roam no more?
We strive in vain to gain that distant goal,
    Our hearts' high hope, our star;
Around our barks the seething waters roll
Seeking that land where peace and plenty are.
Children may find it, but, my weary friends,
For us the quest in disappointment ends.
How shall we reach it? there no oar can guide us
    O'er the mysterious main,
Whose pathless wastes by keel unploughed divide us
    Striving to cross in vain.
The twilight deepens as we dream and wait,
    The night, alas! is nigh:
Our hopes are stricken by the hand of fate,
    The golden fancies die.

SONG.

1.

From friends that deceive me, from cares that perplex,
From doubts that bewilder, mischances that vex,
In the cool summer twilight I sail o'er the sea,
And forget them, my darling, in dreaming of thee;
While the silence around me grows deep as I glide
O'er the moonlit, the magical waters wide.
The silence grows deep and the twilight profound,
But the shore is before me, the haven is found,
And by ways that are secret, and paths that are lone
I seek for thy bowers, my darling, my own!

2.

I have reached them at length, and beside thee I stand,
The dangers are over, the joys are at hand,
And the stars in their silence shine over the sea,
As my darling, my darling! I gaze upon thee.

The daylight divides us, the darkness unites,
The day is all sorrow, the night all delights;
The day that divides us too soon will appear,
The night that unites us will vanish from here,
And the wan moon goes weeping down to her rest
As my darling, my darling ! I sleep on thy breast.

TO A FRIEND.

We wander in the lonely night
    And wild winds rave around us,
Deserted fanes and broken tombs
    On every side surround us ;
Our panting hearts go seeking hopes
    Prophetic of the bright time,
But brambles tear our weary feet
    That stumble in the night time.

We linger in the lonely ways,
    We cast our eyes about us,
We strive to solve the mysteries
    Within us and without us :
We say, " this truth at least we know,"
    We murmur, " surely this is !"
But who that walketh in the night
    Is safe from the abysses ?

We toil and play, we sleep and wake,
    And dream the world progressing ;
We think we leave the curse behind,
    Advancing towards the blessing ;
We travel fast with one by one
    Our hopes in pain departing,
Returning to the self-same point
    Erewhile we left at starting.

But, oh ! dear friend, the days pass on
    Despite our care and sorrow,
And that which seems so dark to day
    Is bright as heaven to-morrow.
The longest journey ends at length,
    We reach our destination ;
And nature grants for every ill
    A perfect compensation.

Oh! dearest friend, if this be so,
    While youth and hope avail us,
We'll work with stedfast heart and mind
    Till life itself shall fail us.
'Tis true we are but exiles here,
    The heirs of doubt and wonder:
The storm is brooding round us, oft
    We hear the noise of thunder;

The lightning tears the midnight sky,
    Our hearts are dull with sorrow,
And no fair angel's hand is seen
    To point us towards to-morrow;
Yet 'tis the weak alone despair,
    The noble hearts and stronger
Raise up new aims from former wrecks,
    And strain and strive the longer.

Our paths, by Fate divided long,
    Has Fate at length united:
New hopes my heart begins to nurse
    Forgetting old ones blighted.
If thou wilt aid me, leal and true,
    We'll take the world together,
And fight the foremost in the fray
    Through all this stormy weather.

We'll strike some blows at those old walls
    Where falsehood reigns securely,
Each blow will let truth's sunshine in
    To shine through darkness purely.
We shall not strive in vain, sweet friend,
    For still through all our losses,
Our hearts remaining fond and true
    Will rise above our crosses.

The sunlight fades, the night falls down,
    Who knows what comes hereafter?
But love can change the stormy world
    To sunshine and to laughter.
Oh! may our hearts, what e'er betide,
    My comrade and my brother,
Be filled with faith and gentleness
    And love of one another.

THE DESCENT OF LUCIFER.

Lucifer, the prince of night,
  From the morning star descended,
Many a rare and radiant gem
Glittered in his diadem,
And his robes were wondrous bright—
  Stars and rainbows blended.

He was weary of his state,
Weary of his glory great,
Of the lore which made him wise ;
He was weary of his throne,
Which was lofty and alone
In the palace of the skies.

Many many years agone,
He went there and dwelt alone
In his solitary pride—
To the mournful morning star—
Exiled out of heaven afar
By a Deity defied.

There he studied many years
The gyrations of the spheres,
  And the scope of nature's laws ;
His supreme and searching mind,
By no faith, no fear confined,
  Did not falter, did not pause,
But unchanging soared along,
  And was noble, if unblest ;
For the truth which made it strong
  Gave, alas ! but little rest.

Down the dark and lonely road
Unto his remote abode,
  Came no step by night or day,
Came no kindly voice to cheer,
Came no loving heart anear,
  Lonely passed his hours away.
His far reaching eyes could see
Back into eternity,
His surpassing strength of soul
Many spirits could control,
But his heart was proud and cold,
In self-worship it grew old.

He would gaze at morn abroad
On the world which owned him lord,
  But no peace of mind he knew ;
" My domain is grand," he cried,
And my range of power is wide,
  But the hopes I hold are few."

He grew weary then at last,
He was saddened and downcast,
  " Oh ! for perfect peace," he said,
" Would to God that I could find
Some serenity of mind,
  Or the slumber of the dead !
It were better far to know
All the bitterness of woe
Which torments mankind below,
  If I so might taste of pleasure,
To endure the smart and loss,
The privation and the cross
  For the hope which gains the treasure."

So he left his home and state,
And his halls of ancient date,
Came unto this earth of ours,
To its sunshine and its flowers,
  To its trees so green and tall ;
And it seemed a little while
He enjoyed his maker's smile,
  As he did before his fall.

Many a month and many a year
Did he wander musing here
  With a discontented mind,
Striving ever to attain
To the peace he sought in vain,
  And the rest he could not find.

He went east and he went west,
But no less he was unblest ;
Wearily the days went by,
Fell the silent twilight round,
Fell the solemn night profound,
And the stars came out on high.

He went east and he went west,
But no less he was unblest ;
" Shall I gain my end ? " he cried,

" I have wasted time and thought
Over knowledge dearly bought ;
All my soul was filled with pride.
Dark and dreary is my lot,
Wisdom now prevaileth not,
    And truth is cold and dry ;
Pride is punished well indeed,
In the bitter hour of need,
By the worm which will not die."

Oh ! how sad and yet how fair,
Seemed the monarch of the air,
As he spake in his despair,
With his dark and lustrous eyes
Looking on the evening skies—
        Far above
        The star of love
Shed its rich and radiant beams,
Shed its calm and holy light,
How prophetically bright,
On that spirit prince of night,
On that dreamer and his dreams.

Lo ! the pilgrim's end is near,
There is one to help him here ;
Lo ! beside the moonlit sea,
Stands the man of Galilee
He the gentle, He the meek,
The supporter of the weak,
He who made our sufferings cease,
He who proved the orphan's friend,
He who did the poor defend,
And was called the Prince of Peace.

" Prince of Peace from heaven afar
Come to where the tumults are,
Come to guide and come to bless,
Point the path of happiness,
    Come to bear the shame and sin,
That the brighter sun may dawn
On this earthly sphere forlorn,
    And the better days begin,
Lowly on my bended knee
I approach and pray to thee,
I who once in impious pride
Heaven and all its powers defied—
I who thought, like God, to be

Infinitely wise and great,
Fallen from my high estate,
Am consumed with misery ;
Thou alone hast power to bless,
Comfort my forlorn distress ! "

*   *   *   *   *   *   •

And the Master's eyes grew dim,
As he silent gazed on him,
As the voice he heard grew faint,
Uttering that sad complaint,
" Prince of Night 'tis well for thee
Thou should'st kneel in agony ;
Fold thy hands and humbly pray,
So the pride shall pass away,
So thine anguished aching breast,
Shall have comfort finding rest.

Underneath the deep blue sky,
While the moon was riding high,
While the murmurs of the sea
Seemed like voices sweet to be,
    From divine eternity,
There he knelt in tears and prayer,
Prince of all the realms of air,
    And the Master knelt beside.
In that hour and in that place,
Came the soothing power of grace,
    Vanquishing the power of pride.

Slowly wore the night away,
Splendid dawned the eastern day,
    Over earth, and sky, and sea,
And the Master raised his head,
" Go in peace, oh ! prince," he said,
" All thy sins are pardoned thee."

Joy makes bright the angels eyes,
Choral strains in Heaven arise,
When the wayward cease to err—
How much more for Lucifer !

LOVE SONG.

———

Life is short and words are idle,
    Who shall say
That the time we waste in labour
    Bounteous hands will soon repay ?
      Cast away
Aims beyond thee, hopes that fool thee ;—
All the wild desires that rule thee
    Make thine aching heart decay.
      Come away!
Where the lamp of true love shineth
    There alone is light,
Where the sacred flame declineth,
    All is sunk in deepest night.
Summer into autumn passes,
    Winter nears us cold and grey,
As the flower that decks the grasses,
    So we pass, and so decay.
      Come away!
Love shall strew thy couch with roses,
    Love shall kiss thee into rest,
Safe is he whose head reposes,
    Nursed on its confiding breast.
Life is short and words are idle,
    All thine earthly work is vain,
Hearts grow dreary, hands aweary,
    All but love must end in pain.

THE SAILOR LAD.

1

He passed at morn along the smiling land,
  At noon he wandered by the lonely shore,
The waves fell laughing on the golden sand,
  And with sweet voices sounding far before
    They called him evermore :
" Why stayest thou in bondage ?   We are free ;
Nor lord, nor law, control the boundless sea."

2

He gazed in transport on its gleaming breast ;
  " Sing me thy songs," he cried, " for I am thine ;
No more ignobly in the town I'll rest,
  Where the thick smoke infects the heaven divine !
    A brighter lot be mine—
To sail away upon the sunny sea,
Like it, be gladsome, and, like it, be free."

3

There passed some weary intervening years,
  The toils and hardships of a stormy time,
Had turned joy's cup to bitterness and tears,
  And the rude tempests, and inclement clime,
    Had spoiled his manhood's prime ;
And now he gazed upon that restless sea—
Hushed were its songs of liberty and glee.

4

Thy promises are false, thy lures a lie,
  Which mock the heart with hopes pursued in vain ;
" I would to God," he cried, with kindling eye,
  " My youth had strived some holier goal to gain,
    Some purer end attain :
The innocent of heart alone are free,
And joyful-minded on the land or sea.

THE ISLAND.

I knew an isle enchanted
In calmest spheres of sea,
Where oft I strayed in childhood
Alone with books to be,
Where oft I wandered dreaming
The dreams most sweet to me.

Some spell of wondrous brightness
It seemed was woven there,
Angelic benedictions
Were in the brooding air,
And all things round were tranquil,
And all things round were fair.

There I with joy retiring
Far from the neighbouring shore,
On greenest moss reclining,
Would o'er some volume pore,
While rays of amber sunshine
Lit up its wondrous lore.

Or where green trees were waving
I wandered musingly,
And gazed on all things round me
With childhood's wondering eye,
The leaves so green and pleasant,
The sky so bright and high.

The pale moons's ghostly crescent
Arose with falling night,
The stars looked down upon me
From heaven's serenest height,
The nightingales around me
Sang sweetly out of sight.

But childhood fleeted by me
And spring-time boyhood fled
And far from that bright island
Alone I wanderèd,
To find that joy was empty,
And peace was with the dead.

Then weary grew my spirit
And pined for other days,
Of this vain world I wearied

And its vexatious ways,
The past alone seemed happy,
Alone deserving praise.

My footsteps homeward turning,
I sought and found once more
The house a child I dwelt in,
The town upon the shore,
The little ocean–island
So beautiful of yore.

Alas! its golden beaches,
Its woodlands deep and green,
How strange and how distorted
Was every former scene,
With crooked streets and narrow,
And houses small and mean.

An hundred barks were plying
From dreary shore to shore,
The solitude of nature
Was gone for evermore,
For mart and railway bartered,
For merchandize and oar.

PREACHERS.

There is a voice in every blade of grass,
There is a sermon in the lowliest flower,
Which all men who are thoughtful, as they pass
May hear at any hour.

There is a parable in every stream,
A voice of warning in the insect's hum,
The hills give answers to the storm which seem
With force like truth to come.

The whispery silence of the deepest night,
The sounds of many waters as they flow,
Are living voices, which when heard aright
Great truths to seekers show.

Then, whensoe'er we ride or walk abroad,
Let us their teachings hear with humble thought,
And afterwards 'twill seem the voice of God
Itself sweet truths hath taught.

ON THE THRESHOLD.

All the golden scenes are fading, night is closing fast around,
Boyhood's sanguine dream of gladness dieth in the dark profound.
Vain I stretch these yearning fingers praying guidance through the dim,
Now the strong world reels beneath me, where is now the angels' hymn ?
All the fairy landscape fails me, gleaming ocean, shore, and sky ;
E'en were brighter worlds beyond it, I could scarcely wish to die.
Here the flowers are blooming sweetly, and the green leaves deck the trees,
And the notes of distant song-birds rise and fall upon the breeze ;
But within the realms of shadow, what existeth who can tell ?
Thence no friendly voices whisper, " Hasten, brother, all is well."
 *   *   *   *   *   *   *   *   *   *

What may mean these drear forebodings ?   What may mean this dark distrust ?
Fleshly weakness, fleshly failings, learn my soul in God to trust !
Though the road which thou must follow leadeth into lands unknown,
He will guard thee, He will guide thee, thou wilt not be left alone.
Like an infant weak and helpless, learn to lean upon His breast,
Thou shalt need no stars for guiding to the havens of thy rest.

SONG

We stood on the rocks which the broad surge vexes
    Under the light of the fitful moon ;
Ah ! why did that fate, so unkind at its kindest,
Allow us to meet when our hopes were the blindest
    Only to part us too soon, too soon.

We stood on the rocks all alone by the ocean,
    And the wan moon waned o'er us at night's dead noon ;
How blest were our hearts as we thought of the morrow,
But the morning dawned over red eyes in their sorrow
    And hearts that were parted too soon, too soon.

The seeds of small scandal bear fruit to destruction,
    Which ripen in poison like roses in June,
And the hearts which for each had all dangers derided
By the falsehood of friendship, behold, are divided,
    Are parted and broken too soon, too soon.

And I stand on the rocks where the wild waves are beating
    Alone in the light of the wintry moon,
While my soul in death's shadow roams onward benighted,
And calls but in vain for the love which had lighted
    Had cold winds not reached it too soon, too soon.

LINES AT SUNSET.

I see the kindly hand of God draw back
The everlasting gateways of the West,
The storm-clouds gather as the sun goes down,
But there suffused and sanctified with light,
There shines the eternal blue. Through the dark world
Of things material the world of light,
The spiritual realms, the home of bliss,
Angelic spheres impinging on our own
Some chosen eyes have seen, and thus found rest.
I gaze in wonder only, and can find
No counterpart of that most perfect peace
In my tired soul, which thirsts, alas ! in vain—
Thirsts for that calm and trustful faith of yore,
Whose mental pleasantness, whose tranquil thoughts
With vernal freshness filled the smiling world.

I gaze in wonder standing awed and still,
The distant voices of the choir divine,
The starry harmonies of heaven afar
Seem floating towards me o'er the gulf of time,
Till all the music of the earth grows dim,
And all the beauty of the natural world
Seems pale and cold, and all the joys of sense
Are but the ghosts which haunt a feverish dream.

Oh ! world unknown beyond the reach of man,
Oh ! heritage of happiness supreme,
The purer moments of the human heart
Are golden glimpses of thy life and light,
Whose frequency expands and lifts the soul
Into communion with divinest things.
But doubt and fear come darkling o'er my mind,
And the wild tides of passion flood the soul
And drain the source of spiritual strength.
The pure ambitions of an earlier time,
The innocence of thought which clothed the trees,
The country lanes, the prospect of the hills,
The open sea, the wide imperial sky
With light and beauty which are not their own,
Are now no more, beyond all hope are lost.
Mine unresponsive heart no answer gives
To gentle calls which came so oft of yore.

The sweet attractions of the nobler life,
The spiritual joy, the heavenly hope—
These all have failed me, and around me cling
This grosser earth, this darkness dense and deep,
Whose pleasures are the dregs of holier bliss.

The sun goes down upon the world ; the night
With all her silent majesty of stars
Resumes her reign, serenity prevails
O'er the whole face of nature ; as of old
The rising moon sheds down her tranquil light.
The vision fails, the voices fade and die,
The tumult only in my soul remains—
My soul which strives among the rocks and gulfs
To find a way through life's mysterious maze,
Fearing full oft lest it should wake and find
The lights gone out, the sacred shrines left bare,
Its paradise made desolate and waste
And overtaken by eternal night.

SONNETS.

I.

When Love's bright flame is kindled in thy breast,
  It shall not faint, it shall not fade, nor die,
  But warm thy heart, and brighten in thine eye,
And beautify the home by it possessed—
Thy sweetest rapture and thy calmest rest,
  Cool shade in heat, shelter when winds go by,
  Resist thou not, nor from thy nature fly,
But, blessing with thy love, with love be blest.
And thou thyself therein shalt find a home
  With chosen friends to hospitably share,
And when the tempest and the lightning come,
  Or biting frosts pervade the wintry air ;
Beneath the shadow of that sacred dome
  Thou shalt lie down, and find thy shelter there.

II.

Oh ! gentle friend, the flowers with June unfold
  And the grape ripens on the orchard wall,
  I would not now foretell the autumnal fall,
Nor following winter's drear unwelcome cold ;
Oh ! cherish while we can life's green and gold,
  But, ah ! for me there is a change in all,
  Sweet voices in the sun-bright distance call,
And heavenly scenes make earth seem pale and old.
Oh ! faithful heart, I would not much complain,
  The birds are singing in the breezy trees,
It matters very little, life is vain,
  Spun out in toil while death alone brings ease.
It is small cause for tears that I must pass,
In life's broad field one withering blade of grass.

III.

Sweet is the sunshine in our youth, and sweet
  Are the green meadows and the wide blue sky ;
  Nature is beautiful, and God seems nigh :
Oft in our wanderings, oft with Him we meet,
His smiles the sunshine and His love the heat,
  And then, oh ! then we should not fear to die.
  We are in Heaven already, for we lie
In summer in some leafy cool retreat,

And gaze in meditative mood on high,
  While streams make mazy music purling by ;
Angelic harmonies our hearing greet,
  And angels pass before the wondering eye,
We seem translated from our earthly seat
  To the high palaces of eternity.

IV.

If thy sweet love be that whereof I dream,
  Bound each to each, dear friend, as day to day,
  I think we twain might wander far away
Where calmest seas in fairy sunlight gleam,
Or 'neath the ghostly moonlight's magic beam,
  Seek other shores where milder laws hold sway;
  Thither, oh ! thither should our footsteps stray
Where all things beautiful and brightest seem.
Those isles of light far in yon western skies
  Swift might we reach in some enchanted bark,
And I would lie and gaze into thine eyes
  Till the whole universe around grew dark,
And sailing through the interstellar sea
Drift dreaming on through dim infinity.

V.

" Tears, idle tears," yet even now they fall,
  Though all the summer morning's sunny hours
  I have been gazing on the meadow flowers,
And the blue sky presiding over all.
I know the world around is bright and fair,
  I know my grief is morbid, wild, and vain,
I know that nature doth her wrongs repair,
  And doth her end desired at length attain,
I know all sorrow must erelong pass by,
  I know these tears are weakness of the will,
But early hopes are fresh in memory,
  And disappointment comes with power to kill,
And fading youth absorbs the strength of love,
And maketh dimness in the stars above.

VI.

Who thinks on life, most sweet our life will find,
  Though much we labour, though we sorrow oft,
  E'en in our chastisements is something soft,
We feel that God in punishment is kind ;
Who tempers to shorn lambs the northern wind,

Who helps the weary up the tall steep hill,
Who leads the lame ones, and who lights the blind,
And doth the hungry with refreshment fill.
Oh ! breathe not that our life accords but ill
With the decrees of all-benevolent mind,
Who looketh upon childhood's simple grace,
 Who presseth lovingly a friend's dear hand,
Whose eyes have known one gently moulded face—
 Dare he call earth aught but a fairy land ?

VII.

Our life is short and wearing fast away :
 There is a hidden music in each word,
 Such music in our purer hours is heard
When in the sunshine of a summer's day,
Under green leaves we hear the brooklets play,
 And, from the pleasant glade wherein we lie,
 Gaze dreaming on the dreaming earth and sky,
And list what ferns and waving grasses say.
It is not, oh ! my drooping friends, decreed
 That we should linger pining here too long ;
God's hand most merciful has sown the seed
 Of swift decay in frames that seem most strong ;
Our feet are blistered and our fingers bleed,
 But all things righted are, however wrong.

VIII.

The sorrow of the heart is like a night
 Which settles starless o'er a sunny day,
And if the moon a moment sheds her light,
 'Tis straightway hid by sullen clouds and gray.
 We are but tombs that cover the decay
Of noble hopes which time had power to blight,
Of golden dreams most beautiful, most bright,
Which fade with childhood's innocence away,
Of cherished purposes sublime and high,
 Conceived in youth, pursued in spite of pain,
Of blighted love whose fondest idols die—
 And only dreary phantoms rise again
Of eyes the lode-stars of our souls of eld,
The lips that kissed us, and the hands that held.

IX.

That is a false philosophy which seeks
 Here by perpetual fasting, prayer, and pain,

Drawn slowly on through all the lengthening weeks,
　　At some far time the happier goal to gain.
Salvation comes not with thy falling tears,
　　Nor laughter checks, nor mirthful smiles delay ;
What value is the gloom of all thy years
　　To Him whose smile is everlasting day ?
Why dost thou linger in the cold and pine,
　　And scourge thy flesh with discipline and rod,
Trust me, oh ! friend, that aching heart of thine
　　Is scourged full often by the hand of God ;
And all thy self-inflicted sufferings here
Will count but little in another sphere.

X.

'Tis not for me to speak of things divine,
　　I am not worthy, as, alas ! I know,
But heavenly hopes most high, dear friend, are thine,
　　And these should help thee in thine hour of woe.
God's hand is laid in blessing on thy head,
　　He guides and guards thee where so e'er thou art,
However fast to-day thy tears are shed,
　　However much to-day thy hopes depart.
His smiles alone can smooth thy gentle brow,
However much perchance it acheth now ;
He, only He, can give thee warmth and light ;
　　He, only He, can ease thy laden breast,
However long may seem this grievous night,
　　However far may be thy home of rest.

XI.

If I should show mine idol to mankind,
　　Would they too worship thee, or scorn and say—
　　"Oh ! sad delusion, this is dust and clay,
And thou, o'erwrought with passion, thou art blind."
'Tis well such pleasure out of clay to find,
　　Such dust to worship, answering when we pray ;
　　I would not worship gold if thou be clay
Nor eyes possess, if I to-day be blind.
I will not show you to the world, my sweet,
　　But build love's temple in secluded ways,
And there bow down and worship at thy feet,
　　And offer thee my meed of prayer and praise :
No stranger foot therein shall entrance gain,
The world's cold strife shall vex without in vain.

XII.

No vestige in the azure heaven is seen,
  To tell us of the sunset's faded light,
  The twilight gathers into deepest night,
And the high stars with watchful eyes serene
Gaze down upon this glade of fairy green :
  The moon's cold beams so wonderful and bright,
  With magic beauty have the leaves bedight,
As she sails on through heaven with stately mien.
The world spreads dimly far before and here
Our destinies divide us. Fare thee well !
  To strive with pitiless decrees is vain ;—
The shadow of an empty hope yet dear
  We cherished ; it has mocked us, and the spell,
  Once broken thus, no power can never weave again.

XIII.

The office of an angel is to preach,
  Of mortals with their fellow men to pray,
  Together waiting for the brighter day
To dawn in the eternal heaven on each.
If all must God for daily bread beseach,
  Shall any, thus made equal, rise and say
  "Concerning this, ye must not," or, " ye may,"
If God hath not commissioned him to teach ?
We all are seekers in our several spheres
  For those great truths which none that know can die,
All seek in different paths with toil and tears,
  If truth should gladden some poor wanderer's eye,
Must those who strive that blissful goal to gain
By different paths be seeking all in vain ?

L'ENVOI.

The early offerings of my life I lay
　To blossom in the shadow of thy feet,
　Should happier stars with influence mild and sweet
The fortunes of my future shape and sway,
Though these erelong must perish quite away,
　It may be I shall come to thee again
　And bring the riper harvest of my brain,
Which may be worthy to outlast a day.
But I am weary with this work of mine,
　Some interval of rest is now my due,
Most pleasantly the sun begins to shine
　In heaven above the beautiful, the blue.
　Oh ! gentle friend, most steadfast, kind and true,
In thy warm arms and pillowed on thy breast
My drooping head finds happiness and rest ;
There let me slumber, there recruit my strength,
Till summer, the desired, arrive at length ;
Then shall we wander forth at eve and morn,
And find new charms this ancient earth adorn
New joys each day invest the varying time
With strength and freshness of eternal prime,
The verdant meads which stretch for many a mile
Shall welcome give with fresh full-hearted smile ;
In ferney glades and woodland bowers of peace,
We'll watch the mellow year's divine increase ;
Much pleasure shall we find and haply gain,
The matter there for many a future strain.

FINIS.

RTHUR E. WAITE.—1. Your verses are more than ordinarily good. Be more careful in your versification. We will insert your poem, as we feel sure many of our readers would like to see them. 2. We believe the book you mention is only published in America.

THE CALL TO WAR.

There comes a sound in the winds around,
 And a roll from the further shore;
The horizon's dark with many a barque;
 'Tis the foemen come to the war.
And the noble must leave the hall,
 And quaff the red wine no more,
For the feast is done, and the war begun,
 And the right of might is law.

The red wine's song shall be changed ere long
 To the brazen trumpets' roar,
And the banqueting hall hear the battle's call,
 And the floor be red with gore.

One night to dream of the blue eye's gleam,
 Of lovely maid or fay,
And then for the sight of the sabres bright,
 With the dawn of morning gray.
One night for priest or monk to shrive
 A whole life's sins away;
One night to chant the psalm and hymn;
 But a singe night to pray.

Then the loud war cry, and the yield or die
 Takes the place for many a day;
And the shout of triumph, pain, and loss,
 And the save himself who may.

The tourney's lance through all fair France
 For a while must be laid down;
And the gallant knight leave mimic fight
 For deeds of more high renown.
The farmer must leave the farm,
 The gallant forsake the town,
And the hunter must quit the spoil,
 And swarm from the mountains down.

For the lion of Albion shakes her mane,
 And the eagle of France has flown,
With her brown broad breast, and plumage drest,
 And her eyes like red coals have shone.

We have raised the flags, and he who lags
 Behind shall *——*——* dare y'uie;
Let knight and lord, draw the gleaming sword,
 And shout for victory.

Hark! from afar rolls the din of war,
 And the wave of death is nigh;
This is not the hour for love's bright power,
 Nor sorrow's regretful sigh.

There's a time for life, and a time for death,
 For smile, and tear-fringed eye,
And a time for peace, and a time for war,
 When the hour of strife is nigh.

Let the trumpets blare, and watch fires glare,
 And pile the arms around;
Let the minstrel's lyre the heart inspire,
 With its stirring sound.

For to-night with ease can we sleep in peace,
 But to-morrow the cold hard ground—
With life-blood red—is our only bed,
 Spite of strife, and pain, and wound;
And a cannon our pall if we nobly fall,
 And to rest beneath a mound.